To See What I See
And Know What I Know

OTHER BOOKS BY NATHANIEL BRANDEN

THE PSYCHOLOGY OF SELF-ESTEEM

BREAKING FREE

THE DISOWNED SELF

"IF YOU COULD HEAR WHAT I CANNOT SAY"

A NATHANIEL BRANDEN ANTHOLOGY
(includes *The Psychology of Self-Esteem, Breaking Free,*
and *The Disowned Self*)

THE PSYCHOLOGY OF ROMANTIC LOVE

THE ROMANTIC LOVE QUESTION & ANSWER BOOK
(with E. Devers Branden)

To See What I See
And Know What I Know

A Guide to Self-Discovery

Nathaniel Branden

BANTAM BOOKS
TORONTO · NEW YORK · LONDON · SYDNEY · AUCKLAND

TO SEE WHAT I SEE
AND KNOW WHAT I KNOW
A Bantam Book / January 1986

Library of Congress Cataloging-in-Publication Data

Branden, Nathaniel.
    To see what I see and know what I know.

    1. Self-perception—Problems, exercises,
etc.   2. Sentence completion test.   I. Title.
BF697.B714   1986   158'.1   85-47792
ISBN 0-553-34235-5

Published simultaneously in the United States and Canada

PRINTED IN THE UNITED STATES OF AMERICA

FG   0 9 8 7 6 5 4 3 2 1

ACKNOWLEDGMENTS

Many thanks to my Bantam editor, Linda Cunningham, whose helpful suggestions and criticisms are a deeply appreciated contribution.

Thanks to my agent, Gerard McCauley, whose counsel and friendship through many, many years have made our relationship unfailingly rewarding.

And finally, once again, my love and thanks to my wife, Devers, who remains my best friend and toughest critic.

Contents

ᚨ Introduction ᚨ

The ideal of self-understanding is at least as old as the great age of Classical Greece—evidenced by the injunction "Know thyself" and the statement "The unexamined life is not worth living." Thoughtful men and women of all times and places have known or intuited that the self is a vast continent, filled with mystery and possibilities for adventure; and eminently as worthy of exploration as the external world. "Who am I?" remains the ultimate question of human existence, and it is a question we are continually challenged to answer anew, as we go on evolving.

We are the only species able to ask such a question; the only species able to ponder our own experience and its possible meaning. We ask: "Where am I going—and why?" "What do I want—and why?" "What does it imply about me that I feel what I feel—or that I do what I do?" We are beings who are able to think—and, most extraordinary of all, to think about ourselves, to question our thoughts, feelings, and behavior. So that, as our life advances, we are able to answer the question "Who am I?" on deeper and deeper levels.

Such, at least, is our potential. But it is an option we can adopt only by choice. We are not compelled to think about ourselves or about anything else. We can move through our existence like sleepwalkers—and this, tragically, is just how much of humanity chooses to live. The result is a chronic condition of self-estrangement and self-alienation. We are chronically lonely—for ourselves. We remain a person we have not chosen to meet.

But in the second half of this century, particularly in the United States, more and more people appear to be finding this state of affairs unacceptable—witness the explosion of interest in the field of psychology; the proliferation of books promising self-illumination; the seminars and workshops aimed at one form or another of self-realization; to say nothing of the increasing numbers of people seeking psychotherapy, not, as a rule, because they are more troubled than the rest of the population but because they are more motivated to become actively involved in the process of their own growth.

In my experience many of the people who enter therapy come not so much because of any specific complaints they might mention at the first interview but with the hope that they will become more intelligible to themselves, more in touch with the sources of their own behavior—in other words, the age-old longing for self-understanding.

Not that self-understanding by itself guarantees successful growth or change. It doesn't. In fact, modern psychotherapy has discarded the belief that understanding by itself is enough. For genuine change and growth, action is needed. But, often, self-understanding is the first step.

And beyond that, self-understanding can be intrinsically rewarding. It can be a source of pleasure. It satisfies our hunger for intelligibility. As such, the experience of self-understanding can be integrative, can bring us closer to the experience of wholeness. And that experience is life-serving.

Sometimes we seek self-understanding with an eye to highly practical and immediate goals: we wish to be more effective in our relationships or more successful in our work, and we want to know if and how we might be standing in our own way. If we find that we do engage in self-sabotaging behavior, we want to know why (for what purpose) and how we can go about changing.

There is still another benefit we can derive from self-knowledge: an enhanced understanding of others. If "How am I to understand myself?" is one of the two most painful questions people struggle with through their lives (with varying degrees of awareness), the other is: "How am I to understand other people?"

The two questions are connected. If we are a mystery to ourselves we tend to find other people a mystery. On the other hand, people who are in reasonably good contact with themselves seem to find others more comprehensible. We need self-awareness and self-knowledge to understand the feelings and behavior of others.

For example, in order to be a competent parent and to understand the emotions and needs of a child, we must be in contact with the child within us, the child we once were. If the child within is a stranger to us, so will be any child we may encounter. If we are alienated from our own capacity for love, or our own need for love, we will not understand the emotion of love in another. If we are cut off from our own excitement, the excitement of others will bewilder or annoy us.

Whether our desire for greater self-knowledge is abstract and general, or urgently specific and immediate, the question is: How can we go about attaining such knowledge? This brings me to the purpose of this book.

My aim is to offer the reader a method of self-understanding with a potential of incalculable power: the sentence-completion technique.

I first developed this technique in the context of psychotherapy, as a tool to facilitate self-discovery, self-expression, and self-healing. To that end, I worked with it not only in individual and group therapy, but also in seminars and workshops, attended by many thousands of people who found they could master the fundamentals of the method rather quickly—even though quite a few started out convinced it was beyond them. Soon it became apparent that men and women, after they had grasped the essentials of the method, could take the technique home and use it on their own, sometimes in very imaginative and creative ways. Later, I began thinking about how I could teach the method to people I would never encounter personally.

I give many examples of how the technique is used therapeutically in several of my earlier books, most notably in *Honoring the Self*, a work that is the most comprehensive distillation of my thinking in psychology to date. However, in *"If You Could Hear What I Cannot Say"* I created my first workbook aimed specifically at teaching readers how they could use sentence completion at home to solve problems in communication with the ones they love. As I have already indicated, my concern in this new workbook is more global: sentence completion as a tool of personal exploration, a means of voyaging into the self.

Let us consider some of the kinds of self-understanding we might achieve through the exercises in this book.

Do you know what situations trigger anger in you, and what you typically do in those situations, and by what means you sometimes try to conceal your anger, and in what disguised form your anger comes out?

Do you know what circumstances stimulate feelings of happiness in you, and what you sometimes do when you are happy, and by what means you sometimes try to conceal your happiness, and why you might feel driven to conceal it?

Do you know how you sometimes sabotage your chances for fulfillment in love, and why you may do so?

Do you know how you may set limits on the degree of success or achievement you will permit yourself, and why you may feel compelled to set limits?

Do you know how, when, and why you become sexually excited, and what you typically do when you do not feel free to express your excitement?

Do you know whether there are situations that stimulate feelings of jealousy or envy, and what you sometimes do under the influence of such emotions, and by what means you may try to conceal or repress them?

Do you know by what means you make yourself anxious or depressed, and how you can change such unwanted feelings?

Do you know the nonverbal messages you received from your mother and father about men, women, sex, and your own body; and what role those messages may play in your subconscious mind as an adult?

Do you know about the child within you, the child you once were, and how you relate to that child, and how that child relates to you, and how that relationship continually affects the rest of your life? Or the teenager within you?

Are you familiar with your sage-self (your higher self), the wisest, most intuitive part of you, the part most intimately acquainted with your deepest needs and best possibilities? What do you know about this self and the role it plays (or can play) in your life?

Every one of these questions, and countless others, can and has been profoundly illuminated by the sentence-completion technique. What this workbook offers is the opportunity to discover and experience this for yourself.

Before proceeding further, perhaps I should emphasize that this book does not come fully into existence until the reader actively participates as coauthor—by doing the exercises. Without this participation it is self-deception to imagine one can really understand what this book provides. This is a book not for passive spectators but for active participants who are willing to discover in the best way possible—namely, through their own experience—how the sentence-completion process can contribute to their lives.

When, in the pages that follow, you read some of the stories of how people achieved major breakthroughs by means of sentence completion, you may be tempted to say, "I could never do that." I have heard that statement many times, made by people just before they proceeded to do what they pronounced themselves unable to do.

As a psychotherapist I see my task as facilitating people's discovery that they know all kinds of things they think they don't know—and can do all kinds of things they think they can't do.

In my view, this is the essence of all effective psychotherapy: to shatter imaginary limits that inhibit our possibilities for aliveness, achievement, love, and joy—to facilitate our discovering how much more we are capable of than we ordinarily recognize.

Sentence-completion work, while only one tool within the wider context of comprehensive psychotherapy, does offer a strikingly effective means of doing a form of therapy on your own, with you yourself as teacher and custodian of your growth.

I welcome this opportunity to show how the process works and, at the same time, respond to the requests of students and colleagues who have asked for more information on how professionals and nonprofessionals alike may utilize the skills this workbook teaches. Let us begin.

Chapter 1

❧ ——————————— ❧

The Power of Sentence Completion

The best way to introduce the sentence-completion process is by telling some stories that involve its use. These stories are taken from my work as a practicing psychotherapist. What makes it possible to report long stretches of dialogue largely verbatim is that almost all of my individual and group therapy sessions are audio-recorded. Each of the individuals in these cases complained of problems that hurt and mystified them, and sentence-completion work played a central role in leading them to demystification and to desired change. They learned to understand themselves better and to make their lives better.

Since this book is concerned with sentence completion as a tool of self-discovery, I have chosen to focus primarily on the process of self-illumination and self-understanding in these stories, rather than on the process of change. The latter is indicated but not examined in depth. Change is a major issue in itself and, to give it the full attention it requires, would distract from our main purpose, so it is treated only as our secondary theme. Here I am chiefly concerned with the process of learning to understand ourselves better, and have selected my case excerpts accordingly.

I think the stories reflect an interesting range of problems. In each instance we encounter a human being who is in pain; who experiences emotions that are puzzling or bewildering; who acts in ways that he or she cannot adequately account for; who is self-alienated; and who, through the use of sentence completion, fairly rapidly achieves a level of self-understanding that sometimes takes months or years to arrive at with the more traditional forms of psychotherapy.

So let us relax and enjoy witnessing how the process works.

It was Janet's first day in group. She was thirty-nine years old, a computer programmer, and separated from her husband after a marriage of twelve years. She remained silent throughout most of the session, which is not unusual for people attending group for the first time. But her face reflected an anguished mixture of pain and fear with (if one looked carefully) a subtle undertone of rage. Finally she asked if she could work on a particular problem that was causing her great distress.

She spoke about her marriage, her increasing sense of misery and alienation from her husband over the years, her lifelong sense of loneliness and isolation, the anxiety she could rarely shake off. "Whenever I feel powerful, it frightens me."

Then she explained that she had recently entered a new relationship with a man, and that she was feeling "very vulnerable and open and scared."

I encouraged her to elaborate, and she continued: "I've been walking around for a couple of weeks telling myself all kinds of reasons why this new relationship won't work, won't last. If only I had never married. If only I were already divorced and everything was long behind me. If only I didn't have three kids. And then I sat down one night and thought that none of these excuses made any sense. If only I could just enjoy what's happening. Be happy. But it's like I don't deserve it."

In earlier books (*The Psychology of Romantic Love* and *Honoring the Self*) I have written about a phenomenon I call "happiness anxiety." It is a problem generally associated with low self-esteem. Self-esteem is the experience that we are competent to cope with the challenges of life and that we are deserving of happiness. When a person of low self-esteem finds him- or herself happy, there is a feeling of inappropriateness about it, the sense that "this is not my destiny, this is not the way my life is supposed to be." So happiness generates anxiety, a feeling of impending calamity. Within five minutes of speaking, Janet seemed to exemplify this problem with almost textbook clarity.

"This is awful," she was saying. "I wanted to . . . I knew that if I came today, I would talk. I've just been putting things off because I'm so scared. I'm ruining my relationship. Crying all the time. Saying things to drive him away."

This, too, fit the pattern. If happiness makes us anxious, if we feel we don't deserve it, a deeper part of our mind—the subconscious—produces a "solution": destroy the happiness. Then the anxiety will diminish.

"Are you in love with this man?" I asked.

"Yes, but I don't want to be."

"You don't want to be?"

"No, because it hurts too much."

She went on to describe how she continually told herself she was going to be hurt; any minute something terrible was going to happen.

When I asked her if the man she loved gave any signs of being a disappointment, she insisted that he was wonderful, the kindest man she had ever known.

"But I'm not supposed to be happy. I just know it."

Her parents had divorced when she was five and she had been raised by her grandparents, who frequently pointed out the sacrifices they were making on her behalf. When she was disobedient, one or the other would say to her, "No wonder your daddy left your mommy. No wonder neither of them hardly ever comes to see you."

Thus it was made clear to her, very early, that she was "bad." She used to wonder how she could make her grandparents, who she described as typically cold and remote, love her; but it seems she never found the way.

Perhaps, I suggested, for a child there had been no way; perhaps the problem was theirs, not hers. She did not respond to this.

She was, she insisted, presently enjoying the most satisfying intimacy she had ever known; but she could not stop crying, could not drive away the sense of impending doom.

"I'd like us to do some sentence-completion work," I said. "Please invite someone in the group to be your partner, then sit on the floor opposite each other, and I'll explain how to proceed." Although the use of a partner is not essential in sentence-completion work, as we shall see, it can be helpful. The simple fact of addressing another living consciousness heightens the reality of the experience, heightens the reality of what one is saying. Allowing another person to hear our thoughts, we sometimes hear them more clearly ourselves.

When Janet was seated on the floor, I said to her partner, "Your job is just to listen. Stay connected with Janet. See her. Let her experience your presence."

To Janet I said, "The essential idea in sentence completion is that I give you an incomplete sentence, and you keep repeating the stem putting a different ending to the sentence each time. Don't worry if each statement is literally true or if one ending conflicts with another. Don't worry if what you say makes sense. You can sort that out later. After a while, I'll give you a different stem and you carry on with that—okay? One more thing: Please don't interrupt yourself once we begin, don't comment on your endings, don't apologize, don't explain—just keep rolling. Look into your partner's eyes and direct all your statements to him."

When sentence completion is done this way, I call it a two-person sentence-completion exercise.

I said to Janet, "Let's begin with the stem **Ever since I was a little girl—**."

She responded as follows. **Ever since I was a little girl—**

I've been miserable.

I've been unhappy.

I've been crazy.

I felt God was punishing me.

I felt Daddy's leaving was my fault.

I cut in: "Fine. Now let's switch to **I learned I wasn't supposed to be happy when—.**"

As instructed, she kept repeating my stem and adding a different ending each time:

I was blamed.

I was left with my grandparents.

I felt guilty.

Guilt to me means—

I'm wrong.

I've been bad.

I'm hated.

no one cares.

people look at me with contempt.

I disobey.

I . . . they let me know I was no good.

If Mother had defended me—

I would have felt loved.

she would have cared.

I would have been important.

I would have mattered to someone.

I would have been happy.

my feelings would be important.

If my father had loved me—

he wouldn't have left my mother.

he would have let me know.

he would have stayed.

I'd have had a father.

If it turns out I am not a bad person and never was—

I don't understand what happened.

nothing makes sense.

it's all been for nothing.

my whole life is a mistake.

I have no family.

I'm on my own.

it's very upsetting to think about.

I don't want to think that.

If I allow myself to be happy—

it won't last.

I don't deserve it.

something terrible will happen.

I'd have to let go of my family.

it would be wonderful.

it would be strange.

the past would be finished.

no one would know what I've been through.

I wouldn't know how to live.

they wouldn't know what they did to me.

they would think everything was okay.

they wouldn't feel guilty.

One of the ways I revenge myself against my family is—

I stay miserable.

I wreck my life.

I talk about my childhood.

I have a rotten love life.

I tell myself I'm unlovable.

I make sure the whole family knows.

It is slowly and reluctantly dawning on me—

I keep myself unhappy.

suffering is familiar.

I want people to see my pain.

I've never given myself a chance.

I'm filled with resentment.

resentment is eating up my life.

I place happiness last.

I like flaunting hurt.

there's a pay-off for my misery.

I don't think I deserve better.

I do think I'm entitled to better.

I could be happy right now.

I could really surrender—and enjoy.

I would like to try that.

I wonder if I'm ready.

nothing's stopping me.

This seemed as much as she could reasonably be expected to absorb at one session, so I paused at this point. (Later she could play back the audio-recording of her work at home, which is something I ask all my clients to do. In fact, I stress the importance of replaying the tape several times.)

"Are any of the things you've been saying true?" I inquired.

"All of it."

I noticed that she evidenced no particular satisfaction with what she had done. To do so would have meant relinquishing, in my presence, a small particle of her unhappiness. However, I imagined that she might congratulate herself later, in private. I complimented her on how well she had done, especially as this was her first time working with me. Then I asked her what she was feeling.

"Like I want to go home, go to bed, cry, get all this crap out of me—and wake up tomorrow happy."

I instantly replied with a new stem. **The good thing about calling my feelings crap is—**

And she responded:

I don't have to deal with it, don't have to let go or change.

Let me make one or two observations about Janet's work.

If adults communicate that a child is "bad," for reasons that may in fact have little or nothing to do with the child's behavior, the child is often caught in a bewildering dilemma. A "good" child is thought to be one who adopts the adults' view of things, who does not dissent or contradict. So if a child wants to be thought good, in order to be loved, and is told that he or she is bad, a painful paradox is generated.

Thus:
I want to be good (so as to be loved);
my parents (grandparents) tell me I'm bad;
a good child does not contradict;
so the way to be good is to be bad.

If I were really to be good, that would make me bad, since important grown-ups told me I am not good, and it is not right to disagree or contradict them. If I am bad, that makes me good, since I am conforming to the grown-ups' view of things. On the other hand, if I were good, that would make me bad—disobedient and noncompliant.

In other words, if I tie my self-esteem to the parents' (grandparents', grown-ups') approval, and the cost of approval is compliance, *then I end up pursuing positive self-esteem by accepting negative self-esteem.*

Thus for Janet to give up the view of herself as bad was both frightening and disorienting; it would be like abandoning a life preserver. But it was this "life preserver" that was causing her to drown in a sea of pain. This clearly was one of the problems that would have to be untangled in her subsequent work.

Her sentence completions pointed to several issues. A poor self-concept leads to happiness anxiety which leads to self-sabotaging behavior. Unhappiness becomes the known, the familiar; whereas happiness is the unknown, the unfamiliar, *the dreaded;* so unhappiness feels more comfortable. Further, we see the motive of revenge: misery flaunted in the face of the family as an expression of hostility and also as a cry for help. (*Now* will you see what you've done to me? *Now* will your heart melt? *Now* will you make me feel lovable?)

I did not imagine that the road ahead would be without difficulties, but she had made a promising start. Cutting through enormous complexities, sentence completion was allowing Janet to discover "who she was." Her work had taken less than half an hour.

"I've come to you for only one reason," said Henry. "I want to know why I procrastinate so much."

I said, "If you want to learn to stop procrastinating that might take two sessions, but if you only want to learn *why* you do it, we can accomplish that today."

"Well, yes, I would like to change . . . I think."

Henry was forty years old, but looked closer to twenty-five. He was employed as an account executive in a large advertising agency. He had been engaged to be married twice, but his reluctance to set a date for the wedding had eventually caused both relationships to end. At work, he left his assignments to the last possible moment, was often late, and was currently in danger of losing his job, even though his superiors told him he performed superbly when he finally delivered. "All my life I've put things off until the pressure is unbearable. Then I go into action. But the stress is awful."

I explained that I wanted him to do sentence completion using me as his partner.

"Let's begin with the stem **The good thing about procrastinating is—.**"

He looked at me in astonishment. "There's *nothing* good about procrastination. What am I supposed to say?"

"Whatever you feel like saying."

The good thing about procrastinating is—

I don't make mistakes.

I don't get criticized for not doing things right.

I can think of ways to be better.

if the work isn't perfect, I have an explanation.

I can't fail.

I can daydream.

I can fantasize being a star.

I feel young.

I'm still getting ready.

my life hasn't really begun yet.

The bad thing about beginning is—

it's a commitment.

it means growing up.

I'm an adult.

I'm responsible.

I can do it wrong.

I might make a mistake.

When I catch myself making a mistake—

I reproach myself.

I tell myself I'm not perfect.

I give myself a hard time.

I suffer.

I imagine I'll be ridiculed.

I imagine I'll be condemned.

I condemn myself.

If I gave myself a right to make mistakes—

I wouldn't procrastinate.

I'd accomplish more.

I'd make fewer mistakes.

I'd have to give up the picture of myself as perfect.

I'd grow up.

I'd enjoy my life.

*I wonder if I'd still be so afraid of
becoming an adult.*

By that I mean—

I'm afraid of dying.

I'm afraid of . . . don't know.

staying young keeps me alive.

young people don't die.

*if your whole life is ahead of you, you're
immortal.*

if you're—what am I saying?

I am becoming aware—

*I get a lot of mileage out of this
problem.*

I'm scared of growing old.

I'm scared of growing up.

I'm scared of dying.

procrastinating puts off death.

this is ridiculous.

I'm going to get old, anyway.

fear of death is taking my life.

I've been kidding myself.

I'm accomplishing nothing.

I know why I procrastinate.

At this point I asked him to pause. "I wonder what your reaction is to what you've been saying," I remarked.

Henry blinked and looked dazed, as if he were awakening from a dream.

I said, "I thought it was pretty interesting."

"It's incredible!"

"In what way?"

"I agree with everything I said. I didn't have to invent anything."

"What does your work say to you?"

"I'm petrified of making mistakes—and of being criticized—so I try to put off commitment as long as I can. Also, I'm afraid of growing up—growing old—I mean, afraid of dying—so I play the eternal kid, which at forty is beginning to feel stupid."

"I wonder what you'll do with this information."

"Well, how do I stop what I've been doing?"

"I wonder."

"What would happen if I just stopped?"

"Do you think you can?"

"Well, I don't see why not."

"Okay, stop."

"Just like that?"

"One day you'll stop—and when you do, it will be just like that. So why not now?"

Of course it was not that simple. But in the weeks that followed he struggled against the impulse to put things off, and in doing so he confronted more profoundly his fear of making mistakes, his fear of losing face in his own eyes and in the eyes of others, and also his fear of death. Procrastination was in part a strategy to achieve immortality—if I do not fully live, I cannot die—a phenomenon I discuss in the chapter on death anxiety in *Honoring the Self*.

By allowing himself fully to confront and experience these fears, rather than disown them, he was able to drain them of their power to control him. In the end he did "just stop" procrastinating, but not before a few last excursions into procrastination. The demystification he desired was achieved during his first session.

Since procrastination is a problem for a great many people, I imagine that more than a few readers will recognize themselves in some of Henry's endings. There are, of course, other possible causes of procrastination: a hunger to live on the edge; a need for the intensity of last minute pressure; a rebellion against authority; anger and defiance against tasks we do not wish to perform. But I cannot recall ever working with a procrastinator who needed more than one session to reach, via sentence completion, the motives of his or her behavior.

It was a new group consisting of eight therapy clients. In order to facilitate our working together freely and openly, I decided to do some sentence-completion work involving the group as a whole.

I explained how sentence completion was done. "The less you think about what you're going to say, the better. You can do your thinking later. I'll give a stem to the person on my immediate left. That person will repeat my stem and put an ending on it. Then the next person will repeat the same stem again and put another ending on it. Then the next person, and so on. At some point, I'll introduce a new stem. Whoever is next in the circle picks up that stem and finishes it, and we continue. And so on."

Someone asked, "Suppose I can't think of anything to say?"

"Invent."

"Even if it makes no sense?"

"Even if it makes no sense."

"I don't think I can do this," someone else remarked.

"Good. Do it anyway," I replied.

Someone protested, "It's not logical."

"You'd be surprised," I answered. "Let's go." There was a rustling of anticipatory tension. "We'll start off with the stem **One of the things I'd like you to know about me is—**."

The person on my left looked uncomfortable, but sighed, repeated my stem—and the process was in motion.

One of the things I'd like you to know about me is—

I don't understand this.

I want to learn.

I'm frightened of what I might say.

I'm a high school teacher.

I'm unhappy in my job.

I don't know what I want out of life.

I get depressed a lot.

I think this is exciting.

One of the things I don't want you to know about me is—

Sometimes I play confused.

I'm angry.

I don't like myself.

I'm concerned about getting fired.

I'm sarcastic.

I'm lonely.

I don't feel much.

I'm very sexual.

All my life—

I've wanted love.

I've wanted to grow up.

I've wanted to be married.

I've doubted who I am.

I've been scared of people.

I've wanted more.

I've been guilty.

I've fantasized a lot.

If I were willing to admit how much I secretly like myself—

you'd be shocked.

I'd feel more honest.

I'd deny it a minute later.

I couldn't feel sorry for myself.

I'd have no excuse.

I couldn't pretend anymore.

what a relief!

I'd have to face the truth.

The good thing about pretending self-dislike is—

I get sympathy.

I don't have to do anything.

it's easy.

it makes me feel moral.

no one accuses you of being conceited.

I deserve it.

people tell me I'm wrong.

it's expected.

If I were more honest about my feelings—

I'd have more self-respect.

I might be disliked.

I might be liked.

I could get more.

I'd feel too vulnerable.

I would get into trouble.

I wouldn't feel so phony.

I'd have a better sex life.

If the tears behind my eyes could speak, they would tell you—

how much I want my father to love me.

I'm very, very hurt.

I'm tired—tired—tired!

I'm ashamed of how I live.

I want to amount to something.

I never had a childhood.

I'm very angry.

I want to be successful.

If I were willing to be vulnerable—

I'd be a different person.

people could know me.

I would have lots to show.

I think I would be liked.

THE POWER
OF SENTENCE
COMPLETION

I'd be more open to hurt.
I'd be shy and frightened at first.
I'd stop pretending.
I'd feel visible.

If I were willing to let you hear the music inside me—

I'd be free.
you'd hear pain.
you'd hear joy.
I could hear it.
it would be dissonant.
I could dance.
I could hear yours.
life would be wonderful.

The scary thing about letting you hear my music is—

you might not like it.
I could sound silly.
I don't know what that would be like.
you'd know me.
you'd be able to hurt me.
I would have to hear it, too.
life would be different.
no more feeling misunderstood.

If I surrender to the process of change—

I won't know myself.
the game is over.
I'd like that.

I couldn't blame or be a victim.

I'd have to be grown up and responsible.

it would be very frightening.

I'd step into the unknown.

I'd be very, very happy.

I am becoming aware—

this isn't so hard.

I know more than I thought.

it feels good to put out what's inside.

my feelings aren't that far from the surface.

I'm not the only person who's scared.

I feel enthusiasm.

I've underestimated what I can do.

I feel more connected with myself.

Right now it's obvious that—

I have more energy.

I feel closer to everyone.

No one's going to ridicule me.

I feel proud of myself.

I feel more relaxed.

yes, I feel less tense, too.

I feel alive.

This is nothing like what I expected.

These three vignettes illustrate some of the ways sentence completion can be used. I think the progression of endings, if studied carefully, speaks for itself and does not need additional comment. We can see that sentence completion facilitates not only self-understanding but also self-disclosure.

I hope by now you are beginning to have a feel for the possibilities of the method. Perhaps the most important point to be grasped thus far is that the way to do it is *to do it,* rather than to speculate about whether you *can* do it.

When we "give ourselves" to sentence completion we enter an altered state of consciousness—we are able to let go of the everyday analytical-worrying-doubting mode of consciousness—and allow another part of the mind, the subconscious, to do its work. As I tell my clients, thinking and analyzing can be fine—but we do them later, as a separate mental activity in a separate context. Often, however, we find that very little analysis is needed, because the material we produce is almost entirely self-explanatory. What we do need, particularly for the generation of change, is to spend significant time simply looking at the endings we produce and *silently meditating on them.* This needs to be emphasized because one of the prime ways we can resist growth is to run from our own sentence completions as quickly as possible, a policy that hardly serves us.

But let us resume our stories.

Robert was a thirty-four-year-old businessman who professed not to understand why "nothing ever goes right for me. Just when my business is really about to take off, I make some stupid mistake to wreck things."

He would forget to return an important phone call, muddle figures on a report; thus causing others to lose confidence in him. On one occasion he flirted outrageously with the wife of a valuable client, with the result that the man grabbed his wife and stomped out of a restaurant, leaving Robert stricken and remorseful.

"All my life I've wanted to be successful," said Robert, "and things always have a way of going wrong for me. I wish I knew why."

I said I would like to explore the problem by means of sentence completion.

"Stand up and face the first person in the circle. Look at that person when you speak. I'll give you a sentence stem; do a different ending with each person. Keep moving around to your right. Remember, if you get stuck—invent. Don't worry if every ending is literally true. Say anything, but keep going. Let's begin with the stem **Ever since I was a boy—.**"

Repeating this stem, he provided the following endings:

I've wanted my parents to love me.

I felt I didn't have the right formula.

I wished my father had amounted to more.

I wanted my mother's understanding and support.

I wanted to be successful.

I've dreamed of making a lot of money.

I've felt weighed down.

When I went out on my own—

I thought, now I'm free.

I felt uncomfortable visiting my folks.

Dad made fun of me.

Mother looked hurt.

I felt afraid.

I wondered if I could make it.

I felt exhilarated and petrified.

I wondered how other people would react.

If I were to become really successful—

it would be great.

I would be happy.

I would be alone.

my family would feel they'd lost me.

my family would disown me.

Dad would feel betrayed.

Mother would say . . . without words . . . "Do you know what you're doing?"

people could be envious.

people could be hostile.

I would stand out.

I would feel alive.

I wouldn't feel so bored.

If my father saw me making a success, I imagine—

he would feel bad about his own life.

he might be happy.

he would feel small.

he would feel competitive.

I would feel competitive.

he might try to get me to do things his way.

he would try to make me feel like a little boy.

he would take the credit for it.

he would be hurt and angry.

If Mother saw me making a success, I imagine—

she would worry.

she would tell me it can't last.

she might start worrying about me.

she would tell me to be careful.

she might be pleased.

she would say "Pride goeth before a fall."

she would tell me how to spend my money.

she'd feel abandoned.

One of the ways I try to win my parents' approval is—

to fail.

to succeed.

to screw up.

to ask advice.

to talk about how tough things are.

looking defeated.

One of the ways I sabotage my career is—

I get careless.

I get anxious.

I do stupid things.

antagonize people I need.

act cocky and turn people off.

forget.

spend money foolishly.

If I were to become successful in spite of myself—

I would be frightened.

I would be lonely.

I would lose my parents.

I'd have to grow up.

I'd be on my own.

I'd be hated.

I wouldn't know what to do.

I would have to know how to function.

The bad thing about growing up is—

I don't know how to.

I'm afraid.

I have to make my own decisions.

I'm responsible.

The good thing about staying young is—

I don't feel alone.

I have a family.

I can tell myself I'm still struggling.

people don't get mad at you.

THE POWER
OF SENTENCE
COMPLETION

By that I mean—

you don't give them cause for envy.

you don't give them cause to respect you, either.

you're not anything.

At the thought of not being anything—

I feel disgusted.

I want to scream.

I want to take a chance.

I feel fed up.

I feel numb.

I feel dead and bored.

I'll never have to take risks.

I've never looked at things like this before.

I've got a right to more.

I always feel dependent.

I've got a right to a life.

I've got a right to try.

I am beginning to suspect—

I've sold myself too cheaply.

I'm afraid to take risks.

I can't even be sure my parents feel the way I imagine they feel.

what they feel can't control me.

I play the victim.

I don't act on what I know.

I like to blame.

if I didn't blame, I'd have to change.

I wouldn't do this to a child of mine.

I care too much what others think.

I want self-respect.

my family and everyone else will have to adjust.

if my success bothers them, too bad.

I'm scared.

this has not been living.

I've got to stop pretending.

At this point I asked him to pause, breathe, notice what he was feeling right now.

"Lighter," he answered. "A weight off me. Optimistic."

I said to him, "I have a homework assignment for you. I want you to make a list of every way you can think of that you might sabotage your career—not only everything you've done in the past but everything you can think of doing—all the ways you could wreck things."

It was obvious from his endings that there were many themes we would subsequently need to explore and work through, but it was not too early, in my judgment, to begin to generate change.

At the next session, when he brought in his typed assignment, I said, "Good. Now attach this to the mirror you shave in front of every morning. And read it—every day. I'll show you how to draw up a weekly record sheet, so you can write down every time you do one of your self-sabotaging routines."

"Suppose this stops me from doing any?" he asked.

"Ah, that's what's interesting. We'll see if you can stand that, or if you have a nervous breakdown. If you do, we'll deal with that."

He did not have a nervous breakdown of course—there was never any question of that—and he did learn (with occasional relapses initially) to give up his career-sabotaging activities. He learned that he could survive success. His relationship with his family was somewhat strained before his success and remained so after his success. They adjusted as best they could. He did not feel motivated to pursue that issue very aggressively and he was content to let his parents' reactions matter less and less, as he grew in self-esteem.

Perhaps I need to mention that a client's fantasies concerning his or her parents' attitudes are by no means infallible. Sometimes those fantasies—along with alleged childhood memories to support them—are

THE POWER
OF SENTENCE
COMPLETION

mistaken. The client's beliefs are to be respected, at least initially, since they are part of the model of reality with which he or she is operating. Later, they may have to be challenged and corrected.

In Robert's case, his understanding of his parents' feelings seemed to be fairly close to the mark. His growth consisted of not allowing those feelings to determine how high he was permitted to rise, which simply means that his growth required a breakthrough into increased autonomy.

One of the central themes of *Honoring the Self* is that a breakthrough into increased autonomy is precisely what the overwhelming majority of human beings need for personal fulfillment and happiness. We can notice the fear of that breakthrough in some of Robert's sentence endings. Perhaps some of us can notice some of our own fears there. But when we finally make the leap, we look back and wonder what it was we feared. We learn we have underestimated our possibilities.

Maria was a forty-four-year-old lawyer, now divorced for over a decade. She had entered therapy to improve her relationships with men. She could never remain in any relationship for very long. Typically her beginnings had great promise. Men found her exciting and romantic; then they lost interest, leaving Maria hurt and bewildered. "You're too nice," more than one man said to her. She professed not to know what that meant, and no one had ever explained.

But today, when she arrived for her private session with me, she announced she did not want to work on that problem, but on "another one—my need for everyone to like me. I'm always trying to impress people. Sometimes I disgust myself."

When I asked her what kinds of things she did to win approval, she said that she understated her income, agreed with the political convictions of whomever she was talking to, laughed at everyone's jokes, and generally tried to sense what others wanted her to say or do, and then proceeded to comply. "All that happens is that my self-respect keeps dropping and dropping. Who am I? What's the real me? Is there a real me?"

After verifying that her tape recorder was running, I told her I wanted to do sentence completion. "We'll take our time today and see what we can discover."

She made herself more comfortable and looked at me expectantly, waiting for the first sentence stem.

Mother speaks through my voice when I tell myself—

you're not enough.

little girls should be seen and not heard.

you'll never make it.

what will the neighbors think?

always try to make a good impression.

you never know what to say.

Father speaks through my voice when I tell myself—

it's a tough world, kid.

the woman who smiles gets more.

the world belongs to men.

if you don't aim too high, you won't be disappointed.

get married and have kids.

Mother gave me a view of myself as—

inadequate.

a loser.

not good enough.

Father gave me a view of myself as—

always on the outside looking in.

kind of pathetic.

inferior.

having potential—maybe.

good, but not good enough.

wishy-washy.

One of the things I had to do to survive was—

hide my rage.

smile.

keep quiet a lot.

look sincere.

try.

*ask a lot of questions I already knew
the answers to.*

learn to do what was expected.

hold myself down.

lock up my energy.

suppress.

practice self-control.

I paused for a moment. "Close your eyes, let it all go, and just breathe
. . . that's right. And allow your subconscious mind to absorb all the
meanings of what you are saying . . . that's right. And meditate, outside
of conscious awareness, on what other solutions might be possible . . . in
the future . . . no need to think about it further . . . just now . . . and you
can open your eyes and we can continue."

One of the things I want out of life is—

to be free.

to be me.

to be successful.

to let my energy out.

to be honest.

to like myself.

not to have to please.

to tell it like it is.

to be independent.

not to care so much about people's reactions.

If I were more open about my own thoughts and feelings—

I'd feel better.

I'd be different.

I'd find out who I am.

I might make people mad at me.

I'd feel cleaner.

people wouldn't matter so much.

I'd see more clearly.

I would grow.

men would respect me.

I lose men's respect when I—

always try to second-guess them.

try to please.

play Miss Nice.

never put out an honest thought.

never put out an honest desire.

never assert myself.

act like a . . . nonperson.

ask them what they want in a nervous voice.

When men turn away from me—

I feel hurt.

I feel rage.

I could kill them.

I want to shout, "Why? I did everything right!"

If men can see my rage—

they can, I know it.

they feel uneasy.

they feel bored.

they feel uninterested.

they want to get away from me.

they feel antagonized.

I began feeling rage when—

I gave in.

I surrendered to Mother.

I never fought for myself.

I never rebelled.

I thought I had to be like Mother or Father.

If it turns out I don't have to be like Mother or Father—

I can belong to me.

my life could begin.

I could be like me.

I could find out who I am.

I'd stop worrying about people.

I'd say what I thought.

I'd earn real respect.

they'd feel rejected.

At the thought of going against my parents' view of things—

it's liberating.

it's frightening.

I feel like laughing.

I feel like jumping up and shouting.

it'd be a whole new ball game.

I'd have my energy back.

I'd know how to talk to people.

I'd know how to talk to men.

Once more I asked her to pause. "How do you feel about your endings?" I asked.

"They feel right."

"And would you really know how to talk to people?"

"Yes! And if I have trouble, that's okay."

"Good. Close your eyes . . . breathe gently and deeply. And meditate on that . . . on everything you've been saying . . . and on the deeper meanings . . . which your subconscious mind can process in its own way . . . opening doors to new possibilities . . . later . . . whenever and however it is best for you."

The reader may wonder what, precisely, I am saying at this point. Very simply, I am laying a foundation for change. By conveying the idea that "at the right time" Maria will be able, at a subconscious level, to process her new learning in such a way that new and better options will occur to her. I say "at a subconscious level" because so many of the integrations that precede growth occur outside of ordinary awareness, although they are usually aided by integrations that are at least partially conscious. It is useful to remember that all healing is ultimately self-healing. A psychotherapist is a coach, a facilitator.

I remarked, "It seems we fell into talking about men today, after all."

"It's all the same issue."

"Seems to be."

"What now?"

"Shall we continue?"

As I learn to listen to my own inner signals—

I realize how much I know.

I feel stronger.

I wonder if I can handle it all.

By that I mean—

(This is a very sophisticated stem which is easier to understand by hearing than by reading. The word *that* is deliberately vague and open-ended. It can refer to almost anything: the statement that immediately preceded the first use of "By that I mean," or any of the succeeding endings, or any other association that arises.)

I'm used to not being happy.

frustration feels natural.

change can be frightening.

how do you live when you can get what you want?

I have so much anger inside.

my anger is humiliation.

I sold myself out.

no wonder I've not liked myself.

When I forgive the child I once was for not knowing what else to do—

I can begin to accept myself.

I can stop what I've been doing.

I can stop hating.

I can get on with things.

I can cry.

I can be a friend to myself.

I can let her be afraid.

When I think about how much I already understand—

I'm amazed.

I'm excited.

I'm inspired.

I wonder what's next.

I want to use what I know.

As my subconscious begins working on all of this—

I feel like it's already begun.

I feel better.

I've got more energy.

I want to start speaking up.

I want to go out into the world—and say, "I'm here!"

I suggested that before we discussed some of the ways Maria might wish to implement her new learning, she should go home and play the cassette recording of this session several times.

I will not discuss the next developments in her therapy as this would take us too far from our immediate purpose here, which is simply to understand how sentence completion can be used for self-understanding.

If you are interested in learning more about the relationship of sentence completion to altered states of consciousness, I suggest you consult my discussion in *"If You Could Hear What I Cannot Say."*

But now it is time to embark on our own adventure in self-discovery through sentence completion.

Chapter 2

❧ ────────── ❧

Guidelines for Sentence-Completion Work

In the sentence-completion work you have been reading, the exercises were done verbally: one individual addressed another, or an entire group. Sentence completion can also be done alone, by talking to yourself in the mirror, using a cassette recorder to record the conversation.

But here we will utilize yet a different form: writing. When working on your own, I prefer this method because it is easy to meditate on the endings when they are directly in front of you.

The basic principle of sentence completion remains the same: keep producing grammatical completions for each stem without worrying whether the endings make sense, are literally true, or are consistent with one another.

Initially some people find this difficult because they feel an obligation to make each ending "the last word" or "the ultimate truth." But all this attitude accomplishes is to block and inhibit the mind.

The freedom to express something untrue is a precondition of the freedom to express something true. This freedom actually releases the knowledge and wisdom ordinarily residing within deeper levels of the mind. And if we restrict ourselves to the surface of consciousness, to that which we already know explicitly, we can hardly expect to grow in self-understanding.

The sentence stems in this book are organized into general categories, each with its own chapter. They should be done in the order in which they are presented.

Ideally, a minimum of one chapter should be completed at a single sitting. But take your time. The goal here is not to finish the book as quickly as possible, but to experience fully each phase of the progression, with ample time for reflection and meditation.

If you are in a close relationship with another person who is doing the workbook at the same time on his or her own, you may wish to meet periodically with this person to share the experience, showing each other what you have written and discussing its implications. Of course this is not obligatory: you may feel that what you are writing is too personal and that you do not wish to show it to anyone. This is a valid option. Further, if you even suspect that showing your endings to someone might inhibit the spontaneity with which you write, keep your privacy.

When doing the sentence completions in the chapters that follow, try to write as rapidly and spontaneously as possible, without censorship or interfering self-criticism.

If, instead of writing, you choose to say the completions aloud to a partner, as was demonstrated in the preceding chapter, the same principle applies. Nothing you write or say is inscribed in stone.

If you do get stuck and your mind goes blank, invent something. Just say anything, no matter how preposterous. Don't give up and stop. Other points to keep in mind are:

• Allow time without distractions or interruptions, so that attention and concentration are undivided.
• Imagine yourself going into a trance to do these sentence completions. (Actually, a trancelike state is the optimal way to work.)
• Accept the fact that some of your completions may conflict with others. Ambivalent feelings are natural.
• Accept the fact that sometimes you have to exaggerate an attitude in order to even get it out at all. Don't necessarily take your statements literally.
• Try to keep your completions relatively short and simple.
• Remember, analysis comes later.

As has been demonstrated by the examples in the previous chapter, we know far more than we are aware of knowing. The challenge for you here is to gain access to that knowledge, to bring it into explicit awareness. Sentence completion is a means to this end.

I should mention that, in the interests of making this book self-contained and complete, I include a few of the sentence stems I introduced in *"If You Could Hear What I Cannot Say,"* or at least stems reminiscent of those stems even if worded somewhat differently. You will find, however, that you cannot do the same sentence-completion exercise twice. Your context is now different. Your experience here cannot be a repetition of any experience you have had before. For all practical purposes, what you do here you do for the first time. If you have worked with my earlier book, you will discover this for yourself.

Chapter 3

𝐞𝟄 ——————————— 𝟄𝐞

Introductory Exercises

The sentence stems in this chapter are provided to give you an opportunity to become familiar and comfortable with the process of sentence-completion work. Beyond that, your endings may generate some fresh insights into "who you are."

On each line below the stem write a different ending. Try to work as rapidly as you can.

You will find it helps to repeat the stem each time in your mind before writing your ending.

And remember, you are doing this for yourself. If you do the exercises honestly, you will be the beneficiary. If you don't, you will be the one who suffers the loss of an opportunity.

Do not leave empty lines. Fill all of them in. Don't tell yourself, after writing two or three endings, "That's all." It isn't. When therapy clients try to tell me that, I answer, "Keep going, please." And they do.

Keep going, please.

As I look back over my life

_____

_____

_____

_____

_____

_____

_____

Ever since I was a child

_____

_____

_____

_____

_____

_____

_____

_____

_____

_____

_____

As a teenager, I

_____

_____

_____

_____

_____

_____

_____

_____

_____

If I ask myself "Who am I?" I answer

_____

_____

_____

_____

_____

_____

_____

_____

Sometimes I give people the impression that I

_____

_____

_____

_____

_____

_____

_____

_____

_____

_____

_____

Sometimes I make it difficult for people to understand me when I

_____

_____

_____

_____

_____

_____

_____

_____

I see life as

_____

_____

_____

_____

_____

_____

_____

_____

I see work as

_____

_____

_____

_____

_____

 _____

_____

_____

_____

_____

_____

_____

I see woman as

_____

_____

_____

_____

_____

_____

_____

_____

_____ 43

I see man as

_____

_____

_____

_____

_____

_____

_____

_____

One of the things I like about myself is

_____

_____

_____

_____

_____

_____

_____

_____

_____

_____

_____

_____

One of the things I dislike about myself is

_____

_____

_____

_____

_____

_____

_____

_____

_____

One of the things I want in a relationship and have rarely or never found is

_____

_____

_____

_____

_____

_____

_____

_____

_____

One of the ways I sometimes contribute to my own frustration is

_____

_____

_____

_____

_____

_____

_____

_____

_____

_____

_____

I am becoming aware

_____

_____

_____

_____

_____

_____

_____

_____

_____

If any of what I am writing is true

_____

_____

_____

_____

_____

_____

_____

_____

This is the place for pause before continuing. Take your time. Absorb what was written. Notice the feelings it evokes, the memories and associations it brings forth. Meditate on what you might learn from this.

❧ *Reflections* ❧

Make some notes on the feelings and thoughts you are experiencing at this point. What issues or problems do you find rising to the surface of awareness? What connections or realizations are beginning to fall into place within your mind?

_____

_____

_____

_____

_____

_____

_____

_____

_____

_____

_____

_____

_____

_____

❧ *Reflections* ❧

_____

_____

_____

_____

_____

_____

_____

_____

_____

_____

_____

_____

_____

_____

_____

_____

_____

_____

Chapter 4

❧ ——————————— ❧

Exploring the Influence of Our Parents

In pursuing a course of self-discovery it is appropriate to go back to a time we may remember only dimly, but which undeniably has relevance to the person we are today. I am speaking of childhood.

In exploring the role of parental influence on subsequent development, the purpose here is not to blame but to understand. We are interested in Mother and Father as they exist in your mind (or fantasies), which may or may not bear a close relationship to reality. And we are interested in how your memories or beliefs about your mother and father might affect your life today. In the subconscious there is only a timeless present where yesterday and today are one.

Naturally the sentence stems provided here will evoke different feelings and responses in different people. There is no one "right" response or answer.

If a particular sentence stem does not seem applicable, does not seem to fit your context, please do it anyway. Allow yourself to be open. Allow yourself to be surprised.

If you were not raised by your biological mother or father, substitute the name of the most appropriate person—a stepmother or stepfather, an older brother or sister, an aunt or uncle—when "mother" or "father" is used in a stem.

Don't decide that you know in advance what your responses will be. You don't. Work as fast as you can. And pay attention to the spots where your blocks or resistances arise; they can teach you a great deal about yourself.

I suggest you resist the temptation to read ahead. Complete the endings for each stem before proceeding to the next.

You should note that words like "always" and "never," when used in sentence stems, are to be understood as figures of speech and not taken literally.

Do not look back and review until you come to the section marked *Reflections.*

❧ *In the Beginning* ❧

As a child, I

_____

_____

_____

_____

_____

_____

_____

_____

One of the ways I felt different from other children was

_____

_____

_____

_____

_____

_____

_____

_____

_____

_____

One of my happiest early memories concerns

_____

_____

_____

_____

_____

_____

_____

_____

_____

One of my unhappiest early memories concerns

_____

_____

_____

_____

_____

_____

_____

_____

_____

The Inner Echoes of Mother

As a child, it seemed to me that Mother was always

_____

_____

_____

_____

_____

_____

_____

_____

As a child, it seemed to me that Mother rarely

_____

_____

_____

_____

_____

_____

_____

_____

As a teenager, it seemed to me that Mother was always

_____

_____

_____

_____

_____

_____

_____

_____

_____

_____

_____

_____

As a teenager, it seemed to me that Mother rarely

_____

_____

_____

_____

_____

_____

_____

_____

_____

As a child, with Mother I felt

_____

_____

_____

_____

_____

_____

_____

_____

As a teenager, with Mother I felt

_____

_____

_____

_____

_____

_____

_____

_____

_____

_____

_____

_____

One of the things I wanted from Mother and couldn't seem to get was

_____

_____

_____

_____

_____

_____

_____

_____

_____

Mother gave me a view of myself as

_____

_____

_____

_____

_____

_____

_____

_____

Mother speaks through my voice when I tell myself
(This may seem very similar to the preceding stem. Nonetheless, do it. It
almost certainly will facilitate your tapping into material the preceding
stem missed.)

_____

_____

_____

_____

_____

_____

_____

_____

_____

_____

_____

When Mother touched me I felt

_____

_____

_____

_____

_____

_____

_____

_____

_____

When Mother saw that I was happy or excited, she

_____

_____

_____

_____

_____

_____

_____

_____

_____

When Mother saw that I was frightened, she

_____

_____

_____

_____

_____

_____

_____

_____

_____

_____

_____

When Mother saw that I was sad or hurting, she

_____

_____

_____

_____

_____

_____

_____

_____

_____

_____

One of the implicit messages I got from Mother was

_____

_____

_____

_____

_____

_____

_____

_____

One of the things I've done to win Mother's love is

_____

_____

_____

_____

_____

_____

_____

_____

_____

_____

_____

When I think of the things I've done to protect my relationship with Mother, I

_____

_____

_____

_____

_____

_____

_____

_____

_____

Today, if Mother saw me in a happy love relationship

_____

_____

_____

_____

_____

_____

_____

_____

Today, if Mother saw me achieving something of importance with my life

_____

_____

_____

_____

_____

_____

_____

_____

_____

When I think of Mother's influence on my life

_____

_____

_____

_____

_____

_____

_____

_____

_____

It's not easy for me to admit that

_____

_____

_____

_____

_____

_____

_____

_____

This is a good time to pause, read over what you have written, and add any additional endings that may occur to you. Remember, your endings don't have to be consistent: one may conflict with another. Don't attempt to judge or moralize about what you have written. Simply meditate on it . . . and on the feelings, thoughts, memories, and associations it evokes.

🍃 *Reflections* 🍃

Take the time here to jot down any reactions or ideas you want to remember about what you have written so far. You are creating a special kind of private journal.

_____

_____

_____

_____

_____

_____

_____

_____

_____

_____

_____

_____

_____

❦ Reflections ❧

The Inner Echoes of Father ⋑

As a child, it seemed to me that Father was always

_____

_____

_____

_____

_____

_____

_____

_____

_____

As a child, it seemed to me that Father rarely

_____

_____

_____

_____

_____

_____

_____

_____

As a teenager, it seemed to me that Father was always

_____

_____

_____

_____

_____

_____

_____

_____

_____

_____

_____

_____

As a teenager, it seemed to me that Father rarely

_____

_____

_____

_____

_____

_____

_____

_____

_____

_____

As a child, with Father I felt

_____

_____

_____

_____

_____

_____

_____

_____

As a teenager, with Father I felt

_____

_____

_____

_____

_____

_____

_____

_____

_____

_____

_____

One of the things I wanted from Father and couldn't seem to get was

_____

_____

_____

_____

_____

_____

_____

_____

_____

Father gave me a view of myself as

_____

_____

_____

_____

_____

_____

_____

_____

Father speaks through my voice when I tell myself

_____

_____

_____

_____

_____

_____

_____

_____

_____

_____

_____

_____

When Father touched me I felt

_____

_____

_____

_____

_____

_____

_____

_____

_____

When Father saw that I was happy or excited, he

_____

_____

_____

_____

_____

_____

_____

_____

When Father saw that I was frightened, he

_____

_____

_____

_____

_____

_____

_____

_____

_____

_____

_____

When Father saw that I was sad or hurting, he

_____

_____

_____

_____

_____

_____

_____

_____

_____

One of the implicit messages I got from Father was

_____

_____

_____

_____

_____

_____

_____

_____

_____

One of the things I've done to win Father's love is

_____

_____

_____

_____

_____

_____

_____

_____

_____

_____

_____

When I think of the things I've done to protect my relationship with Father, I

_____

_____

_____

_____

_____

_____

_____

_____

_____

Today, if Father saw me in a happy love relationship

_____

_____

_____

_____

_____

_____

_____

_____

Today, if Father saw me achieving something of importance with my life

_____

_____

_____

_____

_____

_____

_____

_____

_____

_____

_____

_____

When I think of Father's influence on my life

_____

_____

_____

_____

_____

_____

_____

_____

It's not easy for me to admit that

_____

_____

_____

_____

_____

_____

_____

_____

Pause. Read over your endings. Make any additions that occur to you. Notice your thoughts and feelings. Simply record the tentative inferences or connections that rise to the surface of awareness. To remind you once again: Analysis can come later.

❧ Reflections ❧

❧ Reflections ❧

❧ *Another Perspective* ❧

If I think of my mother as she must have been at the age of five

_____

_____

_____

_____

_____

_____

_____

_____

_____

If I think of my mother as she must have been as a young woman

_____

_____

_____

_____

_____

_____

_____

_____

If I think of my father as he must have been at the age of five

_____

_____

_____

_____

_____

_____

_____

_____

_____

_____

_____

If I think of my father as he must have been as a young man

_____

_____

_____

_____

_____

_____

_____

_____

_____

_____

If it ever turns out I don't need my parents' permission to be happy

_____

_____

_____

_____

_____

_____

_____

_____

If it ever turns out I don't need my parents' permission to successful

_____

_____

_____

_____

_____

Somewhere inside I am becoming aware

If I breathe deeply and allow myself to understand what I have been writing

_____

_____

_____

_____

_____

_____

_____

_____

_____

Reflections

Do not be in a rush to draw "ultimate" conclusions about your parents or about yourself or even about your relationship. Simply note your reactions *as of right now*, allowing for the fact that your experience and your perspective will almost certainly continue to change as you progress through this book.

_____

_____

_____

_____

_____

_____

_____

_____

_____

_____

_____

_____

_____

❧ Reflections ❧

Chapter 5

ᘛ────────────ᘚ

Our Child- and Teenage-Selves

Once upon a time each one of us was a child, and perhaps we do not realize that we carry that child within us, as an aspect of who we are. Sometimes all of us shift into the state of consciousness of the child we once were, and respond to situations in our adult lives as if (for all practical purposes) we were still that child, with his or her values, perspective, and distinctive way of processing experience. Sometimes this can be desirable, for example when we experience the child's spontaneity and playfulness. Sometimes it is undesirable—when we reactivate that child's insecurities, dependency, and limited grasp of the world.

We can make friends with that child, allowing him or her to feel welcome within us. Or we can disown the child, making ourselves unconscious of his or her existence. In this case the child typically proceeds to wreak havoc with our lives in ways that we are unlikely to recognize: making it impossible for us to have a happy love life, leading us to inappropriate behavior at work, denying us the freedom of adult forms of playful enjoyment, and so forth.

If we are aware of the issue of subselves or subpersonalities at all, we are likely to be aware of the phenomenon of a child-self. But I cannot recall a single discussion in the psychological literature of yet another subself, or subpersonality, of the greatest importance: the teenage-self.

Each one of us once was a teenager, and we still carry that teenager within us, as part of who we are, whether we recognize that younger entity or not. If we recognize, befriend, and accept our teenage-self, like our child-self, it can be an invaluable resource of energy, idealism, ambition, and can give us an unlimited sense of life's possibilities. But if repudiated, ignored, disowned, or denied, our teenage-self can lead us to many forms of self-sabotaging behavior. We may find ourselves talking back to the boss in the wrong way and at the wrong moment, or viewing the opposite sex with a teenager's fear and uncertainty, or acting with a teenager's (occasional) lack of good critical judgment, or turning any older person into a repressive parent-figure against whom we feel the need to rebel.

Recognized and integrated, these selves represent magnificent resources that can enrich our lives. Left unrecognized, not understood, ignored, or disowned, these selves can turn into "demons" that obstruct our evolution as well as our enjoyment of existence.

OUR CHILD-
AND TEENAGE-
SELVES

The Child Within

When I was five years old
(Remember, if you get stuck—invent.)

_____

_____

_____

_____

_____

_____

_____

_____

_____

When I was ten years old

_____

_____

_____

_____

_____

_____

_____

If I recall how the world seemed when I was very young

_____

_____

_____

_____

_____

_____

_____

_____

_____

_____

If I recall how people seemed when I was very young

_____

_____

_____

_____

_____

_____

_____

_____

_____

If I recall how life seemed when I was very young

_____

_____

_____

_____

_____

_____

_____

_____

_____

If the child in me could speak, he/she might say

_____

_____

_____

_____

_____

_____

_____

_____

_____

_____

_____

_____

One of the ways I treat my child-self as my mother did is

_____

_____

_____

_____

_____

_____

_____

_____

One of the ways I treat my child-self as my father did is

_____

_____

_____

_____

_____

_____

_____

_____

When the child within feels ignored by me

_____

_____

_____

_____

_____

_____

_____

_____

_____

When the child within feels criticized by me

_____

_____

_____

_____

_____

_____

_____

_____

_____

One of the ways that child sometimes gets me into trouble is

_____

_____

_____

_____

_____

_____

_____

If that child were to feel fully accepted by me

_____

_____

_____

_____

_____

_____

_____

_____

_____

Sometimes, the hard thing about fully accepting the child within is

_____

_____

_____

_____

_____

_____

_____

_____

_____

_____

I would be kinder to the child within if I were to

_____

_____

_____

_____

_____

_____

_____

_____

_____

If I were to listen to the things that child needs to tell me

_____

_____

_____

_____

_____

_____

_____

_____

_____

_____

_____

If I fully accept that child as a valuable part of me

_____

_____

_____

_____

_____

_____

_____

_____

_____

I am becoming aware

_____

_____

_____

_____

_____

_____

_____

_____

When I look at myself from this perspective

_____

_____

_____

_____

_____

_____

_____

_____

_____

_____

_____

_____

One of the most important elements in growth and in self-healing is reconciliation with our child-self, the reintegration of that component into our total self.

We cannot enjoy a well-developed self-esteem while denying and disowning so important a part of who we are.

Reread this section again. See if you can add more endings. You may find this difficult. But persevere.

❧ *Reflections* ❧

_____

_____

_____

_____

_____

_____

_____

_____

_____

_____

_____

_____

_____

_____

_____

❧ Reflections ❧

_____

_____

_____

_____

_____

_____

_____

_____

_____

_____

_____

_____

_____

_____

_____

_____

_____

❧ *The Teenager Within* ❧

When I became a teenager

_____

_____

_____

_____

_____

_____

_____

_____

_____

When I was fourteen years old

_____

_____

_____

_____

_____

_____

_____

_____

_____

When I was sixteen years old

_____

_____

_____

_____

_____

_____

_____

_____

_____ 113

When I entered high school I felt

_____

_____

_____

_____

_____

_____

_____

_____

With my teenage friends I felt

_____

_____

_____

_____

_____

_____

_____

_____

_____

With the opposite sex I felt

_____

_____

_____

_____

_____

_____

_____

_____

_____

When I was eighteen years old

_____

_____

_____

_____

_____

_____

_____

_____

If the teenager within could speak, he/she might say

_____

_____

_____

_____

_____

_____

_____

_____

_____

_____

_____

One of the ways I treat my teenage-self as my mother did is

_____

_____

_____

_____

_____

_____

_____

_____

_____

One of the ways I treat my teenage-self as my father did is

_____

_____

_____

_____

_____

_____

_____

_____

_____

When the teenager within feels ignored by me

_____

_____

_____

_____

_____

_____

_____

_____

_____

_____

When the teenager within feels criticized by me

_____

_____

_____

_____

_____

_____

_____

_____

_____

One of the ways my teenage-self sometimes gets me into trouble is

_____

_____

_____

_____

_____

_____

_____

_____

If my teenage-self felt listened to and respected by me

_____

_____

_____

_____

_____

_____

_____

_____

_____

_____

_____

If my teenage-self felt I had compassion for his/her struggles

_____

_____

_____

_____

_____

_____

_____

_____

_____

_____

If I were responsive to the teenager's needs

_____

_____

_____

_____

_____

_____

_____

_____

One of the ways my teenage-self could contribute to my life is

_____

_____

_____

_____

_____

_____

_____

_____

_____

_____

One of the things I appreciate about my teenage-self is

_____

_____

_____

_____

_____

_____

_____

_____ 123

I am beginning to suspect

_____

_____

_____

_____

_____

_____

_____

_____

If I allow myself to understand what I have been writing

_____

_____

_____

_____

_____

❧ *Reflections* ❧

❧ Reflections ❧

❧ *Integration* ❧

If it turns out that my child-self is an invaluable resource

_____

_____

_____

_____

_____

_____

_____

_____

If it turns out that my teenage-self is an invaluable resource

_____

_____

_____

_____

_____

_____

_____

_____

As I learn to accept these parts of myself

_____

_____

_____

_____

_____

_____

_____

_____

_____

_____

_____

As I think of giving my younger selves what they need from me

_____

_____

_____

_____

_____

_____

_____

_____

_____ 129

As my younger selves learn to feel they can trust me

_____

_____

_____

_____

_____

_____

_____

_____

As I allow myself to feel compassionate toward my younger selves

_____

_____

_____

_____

_____

_____

_____

_____

_____

_____

_____

I am becoming aware

_____

_____

_____

_____

_____

_____

_____

_____

_____

Right now it seems clear that

_____

_____

_____

_____

_____

_____

_____

_____

❧ *Reflections* ❧

❧ Reflections ❧

Chapter 6

Exploring Feelings and Emotions—1

Our feelings and emotions reflect the significance that different aspects of reality have for us. As such, they embody *value judgments*—super-rapid appraisals of "for me" or "against me," "beneficial" or "harmful," based on the way we perceive and interpret the particular facts (or thoughts) to which we are responding. A detailed discussion of the psychology of emotions may be found in an earlier book of mine, *The Disowned Self*. Here we will be concerned with understanding how different feelings and emotions arise, and what we typically do about them and, in some cases, what we might learn to do differently and better.

In working with these sentence completions we want to be as honest and spontaneous as possible—not writing what we think "should" or "ought" to be true for us, but simply recording the endings, however farfetched, however "unreasonable," that surface in awareness as we say the stem to ourselves.

In this chapter we deal with "negative" emotions; in the next, with "positive" ones.

Let me mention once again that, particularly when dealing with emotions, I have had to go over some of the ground I covered in *"If You Could Hear What I Cannot Say."* And yet the overall experience here will be a very different one for you, not only because of the considerable amount of new material I have added, but also because the context is different and so will be the kind of endings that are likely to occur to you.

Pain

I can remember feeling hurt when

_____

_____

_____

_____

_____

_____

_____

_____

_____

Sometimes, today, I feel hurt when

_____

_____

_____

_____

_____

_____

_____

_____

_____

Sometimes, when I am hurt, I

_____

_____

_____

_____

_____

_____

_____

_____

_____

Sometimes I try to hide my hurt by

_____

_____

_____

_____

_____

_____

_____

_____

One of the disguised ways my hurt comes out is

_____

_____

_____

_____

_____

_____

_____

_____

_____

_____

_____

If I were more accepting of my feelings of hurt

_____

_____

_____

_____

_____

_____

_____

_____

_____

If I were willing to be more honest about my feelings of hurt
(I didn't say you're *not* honest, but do the stem, anyway.)

_____

_____

_____

_____

_____

_____

_____

_____

Sometimes the frightening thing about admitting my hurt is

_____

_____

_____

_____

_____

_____

_____

_____

_____

_____

If I were willing to breathe deeply and fully experience my hurt

_____

_____

_____

_____

_____

_____

_____

_____

_____ 141

I am becoming aware

_____

_____

_____

_____

_____

_____

_____

_____

_____

❧ Reflections ❧

If you are tempted to cry to yourself, "But what can I *do* about feelings and emotions that hurt?" my answer is, "Breathe deeply and experience them." Hear what they are trying to tell you. Learn from them. Allow them to have their voice. In experiencing them fully, you will learn to let go of them. It will happen naturally. Trust yourself. As to why and how this process works, as to why and how (as someone said) "the way out is through," I refer you to *Honoring the Self*.

_____

_____

_____

_____

_____

_____

_____

_____

_____

_____

_____

Reflections

❧ *Anger* ❧

I can remember feeling angry when

_____

_____

_____

_____

_____

_____

_____

_____

Sometimes, today, I feel angry when

_____

_____

_____

_____

_____

_____

_____

_____

_____

Sometimes, when I am angry, I

_____

_____

_____

_____

_____

_____

_____

_____

_____

_____

_____

Sometimes I try to hide my anger by

_____

_____

_____

_____

_____

_____

_____

_____

_____

One of the disguised ways my anger comes out is

_____

_____

_____

_____

_____

_____

_____

_____

A better way to deal with my anger might be to

_____

_____

_____

_____

_____

_____

_____

_____

_____

_____

If I were more accepting of my feelings of anger

_____

_____

_____

_____

_____

_____

_____

_____

If I were willing to express my anger honestly and with dignity

_____

_____

_____

_____

_____

_____

_____

_____

Sometimes the frightening thing about showing my anger is

_____

_____

_____

_____

_____

_____

_____

_____

_____

_____

If I were willing to breathe deeply and take responsibility for my anger

_____

_____

_____

_____

_____

_____

_____

_____

_____ 151

I am beginning to suspect

_____

_____

_____

_____

_____

_____

_____

_____

Right now it seems obvious that
(This may seem redundant after the preceding stem, but it isn't, as you
will discover as you allow yourself to continue.)

_____

_____

_____

_____

When we were children, anger, especially anger against our parents, was usually *the* forbidden emotion. "If I were to show my mother my anger, she would not love me. If I were to show my father my anger, he would kill me." So often, at a conscious or subconscious level, the expression of anger is associated either with loss of love or with terrifying retaliation.

Further, many of us were taught that good people are never angry; resentment, we were encouraged to believe, points only to our own deficiencies. Our self-esteem may have become tied to being "above" anger or resentment.

The truth is that there are circumstances under which anger and resentment are perfectly normal emotions. When we deny and repress them, our fear of our own outrage grows worse. The seething urge to erupt, after years of holding ourselves in check, grows more and more frightening to us. It can become associated in our fantasies with going crazy.

In therapy, under safe and controlled conditions, I help clients explore the extremes of their anger, not only because of the direct benefit of emotional release, but also because it is important to discover that anger does not mean (or does not have to mean) irrationality, let alone uncontrollable destructiveness or madness.

In expressing my anger, neither insults nor blows are necessary. Indeed, they are usually the result of denying anger too long.

The expression of anger always means, "I don't like what is happening. I don't like the way I am being treated. (Or: I don't like the way some value of mine is being treated.) There is something here that does violence to me." Underneath there is self-assertion, the protection of my rights, my dignity, my values. And many of us are afraid of self-assertion. We may feel, "Who am I to stick up for myself? Who am I to protest ill-treatment?" So we are led to the central importance of self-esteem, about which I have written so much elsewhere.

Our thinking about anger and resentment should not remain simply on the level of the emotions themselves. We need to go deeper, to think of self-assertion as a willingness to honor our own needs, wants, and dignity; and our unwillingness to be treated with disrespect.

The most important question is not whether or not we feel free to shout. It is whether we speak up at all when we object to how we are being treated.

Speaking up appropriately can be learned only through practice. Sometimes we will speak quietly, sometimes angrily. But the point is to speak—while avoiding attacks on the personal worth of the other individual (which only invites defensiveness and counterattack).

The principle is: Describe what you object to; describe how you feel

153

about it; specify what, if anything, you want done; and omit the insults and personal abuse.

I can be angry at something you have done or failed to do; I can describe disappointment, dismay, fury; I can tell you what I would like you to do; and I can express all of this without telling you that you are a worthless human being (moralizing), that your intention was to hurt me (psychologizing), or that you are just like my previous spouse (character assassination). I do not need to attack your self-esteem.

It is not anger that is harmful in relationships but the moralizing, psychologizing, and attacks on the other person's self-esteem that too often accompany expressions of anger. It is these that we need to learn to let go of. For a more detailed discussion of this issue, see *The Romantic Love Question & Answer Book*.

But for now, reread what you have written on the subject of anger, and then proceed to record your thoughts and feelings.

❧ *Reflections* ❧

_____

_____

_____

_____

_____

_____

_____

_____

_____

Reflections

❦ Fear ❧

I can remember feeling afraid when

_____

_____

_____

_____

_____

_____

_____

_____

_____

Sometimes, today, I feel afraid when

_____

_____

_____

_____

_____

_____

_____

_____

_____

Sometimes, when I feel afraid, I

_____

_____

_____

_____

_____

_____

_____

_____

_____

Sometimes I try to hide feeling afraid by

_____

_____

_____

_____

_____

_____

_____

_____

One of the disguised ways my fear comes out is

_____

_____

_____

_____

_____

_____

_____

_____

_____

A better way to deal with my fear might be to

_____

_____

_____

_____

_____

_____

_____

_____

_____

If I were more accepting of my feelings of fear

_____

_____

_____

_____

_____

_____

_____

_____

If I were more straightforward about handling my fear

_____

_____

_____

_____

_____

_____

_____

_____

_____

_____

Sometimes the difficult thing about letting people see that I am frightened is

_____

_____

_____

_____

_____

_____

_____

_____

_____

_____

If I were willing to breathe deeply and experience my fear fully

_____

_____

_____

_____

_____

_____

_____

_____

I am beginning to suspect

_____

_____

_____

_____

_____

_____

_____

_____

_____

_____

If I allow myself to understand what I've been writing

_____

_____

_____

_____

_____

_____

_____

_____

_____ 163

If my subconscious has been learning more than I yet know
(Here again we encounter a stem that seems much like the preceding one.
But allow yourself to discover where it takes you.)

_____

_____

_____

_____

_____

_____

_____

_____

_____

If I breathe deeply and allow understanding to happen

_____

_____

_____

_____

_____

_____

_____

_____

_____

❧ *Reflections* ❧

You might be surprised by some of the realizations that are coming to you by now. Allow understanding to happen. Allow insights to surface. Realize that at a subconscious level the process of change has already begun.

_____

_____

_____

_____

_____

_____

_____

❧ *Reflections* ❧

❧ *Envy and Jealousy* ❧

If I were to feel envy or jealousy it would be when

_____

_____

_____

_____

_____

_____

_____

_____

_____

If I were to feel envy or jealousy I would probably

_____

_____

_____

_____

_____

_____

_____

_____

_____

If I were feeling envy or jealousy I might tell myself

_____

_____

_____

_____

_____

_____

_____

_____

_____

_____

_____

If I were to be honest with myself about any feelings of envy or jealousy

_____

_____

_____

_____

_____

_____

_____

_____

_____

A good way to deal with feelings of envy and jealousy might be to

_____

_____

_____

_____

_____

_____

_____

_____

As I learn to take responsibility for my feelings

_____

_____

_____

_____

I am becoming aware

As I allow the process of learning to happen

_____

_____

_____

_____

_____

_____

_____

_____

_____

❧ Reflections ❧

Time to look back over all of the road you have traveled in this chapter. You have come a long way. You have a long way to go, but this is a time for rest, review, meditation on what you have written, and contemplation of what new possibilities might be available to you with regard to the understanding and handling of emotions.

_____

_____

_____

_____

_____

_____

_____

_____

_____

_____

_____

_____

Reflections

Chapter 7

Exploring Feelings and Emotions—2

Now let us turn to the realm of "positive" emotion.

❧ *Happiness* ❧

I can remember feeling happy when

_____

_____

_____

_____

_____

_____

_____

_____

Sometimes, today, I feel happy when

_____

_____

_____

_____

_____

_____

_____

_____

Sometimes, when I am happy, I

_____

_____

_____

_____

_____

_____

_____

_____

_____ 177

Sometimes I try to hide my happiness by

_____

_____

_____

_____

_____

_____

_____

_____

One of the disguised ways my happiness comes out is

_____

_____

_____

_____

_____

_____

_____

_____

_____

_____

If I were more accepting of my feelings of happiness
(I didn't say you're *not* accepting, but do the completions, anyway.)

_____

_____

_____

_____

_____

_____

_____

_____

_____

If I were willing to let people see my joy

_____

_____

_____

_____

_____

_____

_____

_____

Sometimes, when I was younger, the frightening thing about letting people see my joy was

_____

_____

_____

_____

_____

_____

_____

_____

_____

_____

_____

_____

Sometimes, today, the frightening thing about letting people see my joy is

_____

_____

_____

_____

_____

_____

_____

_____

_____

If I were to live more fully in the present

_____

_____

_____

_____

_____

_____

_____

_____

_____

If I were willing to breathe deeply and feel my joy without restraint

_____

_____

_____

_____

_____

❧ *Love* ❧

I can remember feeling love when

_____

_____

_____

_____

_____

_____

_____

_____

_____

Sometimes, today, I feel love when

_____

_____

_____

_____

_____

_____

_____

_____

Sometimes, when I feel love, I

_____

_____

_____

_____

_____

_____

_____

_____

_____

_____

Sometimes I try to hide my love by

_____

_____

_____

_____

_____

_____

_____

_____

_____

One of the disguised ways my love comes out is

_____

_____

_____

_____

_____

_____

_____

_____

If I were more accepting of my feelings of love

_____

_____

_____

_____

_____

If I were willing to express my love fully

_____

_____

_____

_____

_____

_____

_____

_____

_____

Sometimes, when I was younger, the frightening thing about fully expressing my love was

_____

_____

_____

_____

_____

_____

_____

_____

Sometimes, today, the frightening thing about fully expressing my love is

_____

_____

_____

_____

_____

_____

_____

_____

_____

If I were willing to breathe deeply and feel my love fully

_____

_____

_____

_____

_____

_____

_____

The tragedy of so many people's lives is that they are more concerned with avoiding hurt (or rejection) than with experiencing joy (or love). The avoidance of the negative matters more to them than the attainment of the positive. But of course such a policy makes pain and disappointment inevitable; they become the saboteurs of their own happiness.

Might any of this apply to you?

Reread your endings for this section and then proceed with your notes.

Reflections

❧ *Reflections* ❧

❦ *Feeling Loved* ❧

I can remember feeling loved when

_____

_____

_____

_____

_____

_____

_____

_____

_____

Sometimes, today, I feel loved when

_____

_____

_____

_____

_____

_____

_____

_____

Sometimes, when I feel loved, I

_____

_____

_____

_____

_____

_____

_____

_____

Sometimes I try to deny feeling loved by

_____

_____

_____

_____

_____

_____

_____

_____

If I were more accepting when I feel loved

_____

_____

_____

_____

_____

_____

_____

_____

_____

_____

_____

If I were willing to let others see that I feel loved

_____

_____

_____

_____

_____

_____

_____

_____

_____

Sometimes the frightening thing about admitting I feel loved is

_____

_____

_____

_____

_____

_____

_____

_____

If I were willing to breathe deeply and let myself feel loved

_____

_____

_____

_____

_____

_____

_____

_____

_____

_____

I am becoming aware

_____

_____

_____

_____

_____

_____

_____

_____

_____

I am beginning to suspect

_____

_____

_____

_____

_____

_____

_____

_____

If people knew how much love I have locked up inside of me

_____

_____

_____

_____

_____

❧ Reflections ❧

❧ Reflections ❧

Reflections

❧ Excitement ❧

"Excitement" can be about life, about a project, about another person, about myself.

Sometimes I feel excited when

_____

_____

_____

_____

_____

_____

_____

_____

Sometimes, when I feel excited, I

_____

_____

_____

_____

_____

_____

_____

_____

Sometimes I try to hide my excitement by
(Do not tell yourself "I cannot relate to this." _Everyone_ sometimes tries to appear calm, indifferent, or "cool," while inwardly bursting with excitement—perhaps when first meeting an attractive person of the opposite sex or when hearing an appealing job offer. In any event, if you get stuck—invent something. I challenge you to do ten endings (rapidly) without saying anything true about yourself.)

_____

_____

_____

_____

_____

_____

_____

_____

_____

_____

One of the disguised ways my excitement comes out is

_____

_____

_____

_____

_____

_____

_____

_____

_____

If I were more accepting of my feelings of excitement

_____

_____

_____

_____

_____

_____

_____

_____

If I were willing to let people see my excitement

_____

_____

_____

_____

_____

_____

_____

_____

_____

_____

_____

Sometimes, when I was younger, the frightening thing about showing my excitement was

_____

_____

_____

_____

_____

_____

_____

_____

_____

Sometimes, today, the frightening thing about showing my excitement is

_____

_____

_____

_____

_____

_____

_____

_____

If I were willing to breathe deeply and fully experience my excitement

_____

_____

_____

_____

_____

_____

_____

_____

_____

_____

I am becoming aware

_____

_____

_____

_____

_____

_____

_____

_____

_____

As more and more understanding happens at a subconscious level

_____

_____

_____

_____

_____

_____

_____

_____

If, indeed, I am learning more than I yet recognize

_____

_____

_____

_____

_____

_____

_____

_____

_____

❧ *Reflections* ❧

The truth is that nothing is more precious or valuable than our ability to experience excitement, since this ultimately means our ability to respond positively to the possibilities of life.

No trait is more beautiful in a child—or more admirable in an old person.

Our ability to experience excitement should be our most protected and nurtured possession.

_____

_____

_____

_____

_____

_____

_____

❧ Reflections ❧

_____

_____

_____

_____

_____

_____

_____

_____

_____

_____

_____

_____

_____

_____

_____

Chapter 8

Exploring Sexuality

In this chapter we will use sentence completion to deepen our understanding of our sexual psychology. Let me say, once again, that you should think of this as a private journal you are creating.

Nothing you write is engraved in stone. Sentence completion is a vehicle of exploration and discovery that accommodates errors, false starts, thinking aloud, and so forth. But if you persevere, in the end you will know what endings are most valuable and illuminating for you—and your subconscious mind will know even more.

❧ *Sexuality* ❧

Sometimes I feel sexually inspired ("turned on") when

_____

_____

_____

_____

_____

_____

_____

_____

_____

Sometimes, when I'm feeling sexual, I

_____

_____

_____

_____

_____

_____

_____

_____

_____

_____

One of the ways I sometimes hide my sexual excitement is

_____

_____

_____

_____

_____

_____

_____

_____

_____

One of the ways my sexual excitement comes out is

_____

_____

_____

_____

_____

_____

_____

_____

_____

If I were fully comfortable with my sexuality
(I am not suggesting you are not comfortable; do it, anyway.)

_____

_____

_____

_____

_____

_____

_____

_____

_____

_____

_____

If I were fully honest with myself about my sexual feelings
(Again, this stem appears very much like the preceding one, but do it, anyway. Work rapidly here. See what emerges.)

_____

_____

_____

_____

_____

_____

_____

_____

_____ 215

A better way to deal with my sexuality might be to

_____

_____

_____

_____

_____

_____

_____

_____

❧ *Reflections* ❧

_____

_____

_____

_____

_____

❧ Reflections ❧

❧ *Parental Influences on Sexuality* ❧

In a previous chapter we looked at parental influences in general. Here, we want to consider specifically the area of our sexuality. It seemed appropriate to reserve the following stems for this chapter in order to facilitate a more integrated perspective on our sexual psychology.

   If you have already worked in *"If You Could Hear What I Cannot Say,"* you may notice that I have had to recapitulate some stems from that book. However, I think you will find your experience very different here. To say it once more: Your context is now different, you are at another stage of development precisely because you have done the other work. And if you have not worked with *"If You Could Hear. . ."* and choose to proceed to that book from this one, the same logic applied: A new adventure, with new possibilities of discovery, awaits you.

As a child, it seemed to me that Mother gave me the feeling my body was

_____

_____

_____

_____

_____

_____

_____

As a teenager, it seemed to me that Mother gave me the feeling my body was

_____

_____

_____

_____

_____

_____

_____

_____

_____

When I was growing up, Mother gave me the feeling that sex was

_____

_____

_____

_____

_____

_____

_____

_____

Mother gave me the feeling that women are

_____

_____

_____

_____

_____

_____

_____

_____

_____

_____

Mother gave me the feeling that men are

_____

_____

_____

_____

_____

_____

_____

_____

_____ 221

Mother gave me the feeling that love is

_____

_____

_____

_____

_____

_____

_____

_____

As a child, it seemed to me that Father gave me the feeling my body was

_____

_____

_____

_____

_____

_____

_____

_____

_____

_____

As a teenager, it seemed to me that Father gave me the feeling my body was

_____

_____

_____

_____

_____

_____

_____

_____

_____

When I was growing up, Father gave me the feeling that sex was

_____

_____

_____

_____

_____

_____

_____

_____

Father gave me the feeling that women are

_____

_____

_____

_____

_____

_____

_____

_____

_____

_____

_____

Father gave me the feeling that men are

_____

_____

_____

_____

_____

_____

_____

_____

_____ 225

Father gave me the feeling that love is

_____

_____

_____

_____

_____

_____

_____

_____

_____

I am becoming aware

_____

_____

_____

_____

_____

_____

_____

_____

_____

_____

_____

If I were completely free of Mother's sexual influence

_____

_____

_____

_____

_____

_____

_____

_____

_____

If I were completely free of Father's sexual influence

_____

_____

_____

_____

_____

_____

_____

_____

If I listen to my own inner voice rather than the voice of Mother or Father

_____

_____

_____

_____

_____

_____

_____

_____

_____

_____

_____

If I allow myself to see what I see, and know what I know

_____

_____

_____

_____

_____

_____

_____

_____

_____

_____ 229

If no one has the right to dictate my sexuality

_____

_____

_____

_____

_____

_____

_____

_____

If I were willing to take full responsibility for my own sexuality

_____

_____

_____

_____

_____

_____

_____

_____

_____

_____

The frightening thing about taking full responsibility for my sexuality is

_____

_____

_____

_____

_____

_____

_____

_____

The liberating thing about taking full responsibility for my sexuality is

_____

_____

_____

_____

_____

_____

_____

_____

❧ *Reflections* ❧

Time to pause. Allow yourself to meditate on what you have written in this section. What thoughts and feelings are stirred up in you?

_____

_____

_____

_____

Reflections

233

❧ *The Opposite Sex* ❧

The next two stems resemble stems you did early in this book. The repetition is intentional. Do not look back. You are learning, growing, and evolving even as you write. Work as rapidly as possible here.

Woman to me is

_____

_____

_____

_____

_____

_____

_____

_____

Man to me is

_____

_____

_____

_____

_____

_____

_____

_____

_____

_____

The hard thing about being a woman is
(Do this stem, regardless of your own gender.)

_____

_____

_____

_____

_____

_____

_____

_____

The hard thing about being a man is
(Do this stem, regardless of your own gender.)

_____

_____

_____

_____

_____

_____

_____

_____

(This stem is for men.)

If I didn't have to be concerned about being masculine

_____

_____

_____

_____

_____

_____

_____

_____

_____

(This stem is for women.)

If I didn't have to be concerned about being feminine

_____

_____

_____

_____

_____

_____

_____

_____

_____

_____ 237

(This stem is for men.)

If it turns out woman is my other self
(Do not pause too long to ponder what the stem means. I assure you, somewhere inside you know. All of us contain an opposite-gender sub-personality: every male contains a female component, or subself; every female contains a male component, or subself.)

_____

_____

_____

_____

_____

_____

_____

_____

(This stem is for women.)

If it turns out man is my other self

_____

_____

_____

I am becoming aware

As I allow myself to understand what I have been writing

_____

_____

_____

_____

_____

_____

_____

_____

_____

❧ *Reflections* ❧

Often we do violence to who we are because of misguided notions of "masculinity" and "femininity." We attempt to disown whatever does not fit our image of what is appropriate.

Thus, men often disown tenderness, sensuality, their ability to be nurturing, just as women often disown strength, assertiveness, sexuality, their ability to be self-reliant.

Where do you stand on these issues? What can you learn about yourself from your endings thus far? Is it time to rethink some of your assumptions about maleness and femaleness?

_____

_____

_____

_____

_____

_____

_____

_____

_____

_____

_____

_____

❧ *Reflections* ❧

Sex and Spirit

If there is a respect in which my sexuality expresses my deepest self

_____

_____

_____

_____

_____

_____

_____

_____

_____

If I take full responsibility for my sexual choices and actions

_____

_____

_____

_____

_____

_____

_____

_____

If I look at my sexual partner and tell myself, "He/she is _my_ choice"

_____

_____

_____

_____

_____

_____

_____

_____

_____

    What changes for us, then, as we begin to understand that body and spirit are one?

    What if it is self-delusion to imagine that our sex life bears little or no relation to the rest of who and what we are?

    And if we do learn to see sex as an act of self-expression, what follows?

I am becoming aware

_____

_____

_____

_____

_____

_____

_____

_____

_____

The difficult thing about looking clearly at this issue is
(You don't find it difficult? Do the stem, anyway.)

_____

_____

_____

_____

_____

_____

_____

_____

The liberating thing about looking at this issue clearly might be

_____

_____

_____

_____

Reflections

❦ *Reflections* ❧

Chapter 9

Self-Esteem

Positive self-esteem is our deepest psychological need. By "self-esteem," I mean our experience of being competent to deal with the challenges of life and of being deserving of happiness. I cannot think of a single major psychological problem—from fear of intimacy or of success, to under-achievement at school or at work, to anxiety or depression, to alcohol abuse or drug addiction, to child molesting or spouse battering, to suicide or crimes of violence—that is not traceable to a poor self-concept. Of all the judgments we pass in life, none is as important as the one we pass on ourselves. Our self-concept tends to be our destiny.

I have written at length on this subject in *Honoring the Self* and before that in *The Psychology of Self-Esteem*. This is not the place for a general discussion of the nature of self-esteem and its role in human life. But I do want to stress that self-esteem is a function of our deepest feelings about ourselves; it is not a matter of particular skills or particular knowledge. It is certainly not a matter of how well-liked we are. It is a matter of the extent to which we experience ourselves as appropriate to life and to the requirements of life.

We may think of self-esteem as the experience that we are *competent* to live and *worthy* of happiness.

The experience that I am competent to live means confidence in the functioning of my mind; in my ability to understand and judge the facts of reality within the sphere of my interests and needs; intellectual self-trust; intellectual self-reliance.

The experience that I am worthy of happiness means an affirmative attitude toward my right to a joyful existence; an affirmative attitude toward the assertion of my wants and needs; self-acceptance and self-respect; the feeling that happiness is my natural birthright.

The possibility of developing a healthy self-esteem is inherent in our nature, since our ability to think is the basic source of competence, and the fact that we are alive is the basic source of our right to strive for happiness.

But in the process of growing up, and in the process of living itself, it is possible for us to become alienated from our self-esteem. We may lose our best vision of ourselves, because of negative messages absorbed from others, and/or because of our own defaults on honesty, integrity, and self-responsibility.

I have never met anyone entirely lacking in self-esteem and I have never met anyone who could not grow in self-esteem. And the level of our self-esteem affects virtually every aspect of our existence.

Early Messages

Having done so much work on childhood earlier in this book, you should be able to move very rapidly in this opening section, without thinking about what you wrote before.

Mother gave me the sense that I was

_____

_____

_____

_____

_____

_____

_____

_____

_____

Father gave me the sense that I was

_____

_____

_____

_____

_____

_____

_____

_____

When Mother saw me making mistakes, she

_____

_____

_____

_____

_____

When Father saw me making mistakes, he

When I see myself making mistakes, I

_____

_____

_____

_____

_____

_____

_____

_____

If someone had fully believed in my intelligence

_____

_____

_____

_____

_____

_____

If someone had fully believed in my goodness

One of the messages about myself I absorbed in childhood was that I
(Of course you have covered this ground from a variety of angles already.
Working very rapidly, notice what feels most important to write down at
this moment and in this context.)

_____

_____

_____

_____

_____

_____

_____

_____

I am becoming aware

_____

_____

_____

_____

_____

❧ Reflections ❧

_____

_____

_____

_____

_____

_____

_____

_____

_____

_____

_____

_____

_____

_____

_____

_____

_____

❧ *Reflections* ❧

❧ *Behaviors That Affect Self-Esteem* ❧

Sometimes I hurt my self-esteem when I

_____

_____

_____

_____

_____

_____

_____

_____

_____

I like myself most when I

_____

_____

_____

_____

_____

_____

_____

_____

I like myself most when, in dealing with others, I

_____

_____

_____

_____

_____

_____

_____

_____

_____

_____

When I choose to function consciously and think about what I am doing

_____

_____

_____

_____

_____

_____

_____

_____

_____

When I am dishonest with myself or others

_____

_____

_____

_____

_____

_____

_____

_____

When I am honest with myself or others

_____

_____

_____

_____

_____

_____

_____

_____

_____

_____

_____

When I act with integrity

_____

_____

_____

_____

_____

_____

_____

_____

_____

If I say "no" when I want to say "no," and "yes" when I want to say "yes"

_____

_____

_____

_____

_____

_____

_____

_____

_____

When I take full responsibility for every word I utter

_____

_____

_____

_____

_____

_____

_____

_____

_____

_____

_____

If I allow myself to understand what I am writing

_____

_____

_____

_____

_____

_____

_____

_____

_____

_____ 265

❧ Reflections ❧

Reflections

❧ Self-Sabotage ❧

One of the ways I sometimes contribute to my own frustration is

_____

_____

_____

_____

_____

_____

_____

_____

_____

One of the ways I sometimes make it difficult for people to give me what I want is

_____

_____

_____

_____

_____

_____

_____

_____

_____

One of the ways I sometimes obstruct my own success is

_____

_____

_____

_____

_____

_____

_____

_____

_____ 269

One of the ways I sometimes make myself helpless is

_____

_____

_____

_____

_____

_____

_____

_____

_____

The good thing about making myself helpless is
(I know, I know, but do it, anyway.)

_____

_____

_____

_____

_____

_____

_____

_____

_____

_____

If I were to take full responsibility for my own existence

_____

_____

_____

_____

_____

_____

_____

_____

_____

If I were to take full responsibility for getting what I want

_____

_____

_____

_____

_____

_____

_____

_____

_____

If I fully accepted my right to be happy

_____

_____

_____

_____

_____

_____

_____

_____

_____

_____

_____

I am becoming aware

_____

_____

_____

_____

_____

_____

_____

_____

_____

_____ 273

If I allow myself to understand what I have been writing

_____

_____

_____

_____

_____

_____

_____

_____

❧ *Reflections* ❧

_____

_____

_____

_____

_____

Reflections

❧ Waking Up ❧

If I exercise the courage to honor my own life

_____

_____

_____

_____

_____

_____

_____

_____

_____

If I were willing to see what I see, and know what I know

_____

_____

_____

_____

_____

_____

_____

_____

_____

If I were willing to breathe deeply and feel my own power

_____

_____

_____

_____

_____

_____

_____

_____

_____

If I allow old wounds to fade away

_____

_____

_____

_____

_____

_____

_____

_____

If I allow myself to wake up to the possibilities of life

_____

_____

_____

_____

_____

_____

_____

_____

_____

_____

If I stop blaming others and start living

_____

_____

_____

_____

_____

_____

_____

_____

_____

If I stop looking for someone to feel sorry for me

_____

_____

_____

_____

_____

_____

_____

_____

If I had the courage to honor my own excitement

_____

_____

_____

_____

_____

_____

_____

_____

_____

_____

As I allow myself to feel lighter

_____

_____

_____

_____

_____

_____

_____

_____

_____

❧ Reflections ❧

❧ Reflections ❧

❧ Self-Acceptance ❧

If self-acceptance means not denying or disowning who I am

_____

_____

_____

_____

_____

_____

_____

_____

_____

_____

If self-acceptance is the foundation of good self-esteem

_____

_____

_____

_____

_____

_____

_____

_____

_____

_____

As I learn to accept my feelings whether I like them or not

_____

_____

_____

_____

_____

_____

_____

_____

_____

As I learn to accept all the different parts of who I am

_____

_____

_____

_____

_____

_____

_____

_____

As I breathe into feelings rather than pretend I don't feel them

_____

_____

_____

_____

_____

_____

_____

_____

_____

_____

As I admit how much I secretly (or not so secretly) like myself

_____

_____

_____

_____

_____

_____

_____

_____

_____

If I surrender to the process of change and growth

_____

_____

_____

_____

_____

_____

_____

_____

As I become more serene

_____

_____

_____

_____

_____

_____

_____

_____

_____

_____

_____

As I feel energy flowing through my body

_____

_____

_____

_____

_____

_____

_____

_____

_____ 289

As this work changes me in ways I have not fully noticed

_____

_____

_____

_____

_____

_____

_____

_____

I am becoming aware

_____

_____

_____

_____

_____

_____

_____

_____

_____

❧ *Reflections* ❧

_____

_____

_____

_____

_____

_____

_____

_____

_____

_____

_____

_____

Reflections

Chapter 10

The Sage-Self

In doing psychotherapy I find it useful to work with the concept of a sage-self (or higher self)—a part of our psyche that is much wiser than the rest of us, much more in contact with our deepest needs and best possibilities. It is a powerful metaphor, and perhaps a bit more than a metaphor.

All of us have known moments of extraordinary lucidity when ordinary limitations and constraints seem to fall away. We can look objectively at our lives, and experience what is truly important, with almost supernormal clarity. I call that perspective the sage-self.

We seem to know intuitively that if we could live our lives from that state of consciousness we would be transformed. It seems as if we are given glimpses of a higher order of consciousness, almost as a preview of the next stage of our evolution.

I think that sometimes the sage-self appears when we are doing sentence completion—when we are *really* doing it, giving ourselves entirely to the process, without inhibition or restraint; and we are awed by a wisdom we did not know we possessed. It is a level of wisdom that does not ordinarily exist in that suboptimal state we call everyday awareness. It exists deep within us, and—here is the point—the challenge is how to gain access to that wisdom with some consistency.

Sentence completion is not a total answer, but it can help. For many people it is the doorway through which they can enter this realm of higher possibilities that already exists within their own psyche.

I offer that doorway to you.

Contacting Your Higher Self

If there is a part of me that knows more than my conscious mind

_____

_____

_____

_____

_____

_____

_____

_____

Sometimes, when I am alone and see my life with my own eyes

_____

_____

_____

_____

_____

_____

_____

_____

When I feel connected with what really matters to me

_____

_____

_____

_____

_____

_____

_____

_____

When I think of all the nonsense I allow to clutter up my vision

_____

_____

_____

_____

_____

_____

_____

As I rise higher and higher above concerns that are not really what life is about

_____

_____

_____

_____

_____

_____

_____

_____

_____

_____

When I look at my childhood from the perspective of my higher self

_____

_____

_____

_____

_____

_____

_____

_____

_____ 297

When I rise above fighting myself or blaming others

_____

_____

_____

_____

_____

_____

_____

_____

When I understand that all that exists is the present

_____

_____

_____

_____

_____

_____

_____

_____

_____

_____

_____

When I allow myself to experience the ecstatic part of me

_____

_____

_____

_____

_____

_____

_____

_____

_____

I am becoming aware

_____

_____

_____

_____

_____

_____

_____

_____

As my subconscious mind absorbs everything I have been writing

_____

_____

_____

_____

_____

_____

_____

_____

_____

_____

As these understandings become more and more a part of me

_____

_____

_____

_____

_____

_____

_____

_____

_____ 301

❧ *Reflections* ❧

If you have done the exercises to this point, in the way I have recom-
mended, the process of change has already been generated within you,
and will continue long after you put this book down. But take your time
here to meditate on what you have written in the preceding section. What
does it say to you? What have you learned?

_____

_____

_____

_____

_____

_____

_____

_____

_____

_____

_____

_____

Reflections

The Triumph of Self-Esteem ❧

Here you will find a number of rather similar stems. But do each of them. The process of writing each set of endings helps facilitate growth, learning, and change.

As I learn to hear the voice of my sage-self

_____

_____

_____

_____

_____

_____

_____

As I become more sensitive to the things a deeper part of me knows

_____

_____

_____

_____

_____

_____

As I learn to honor my own wisdom

_____

_____

_____

_____

_____

_____

_____

_____

As I gain the courage to live from the perspective of my sage-self

_____

_____

_____

_____

_____

_____

_____

_____

If my best and clearest moments turn out to be what life is really all about

_____

_____

_____

_____

_____

_____

_____

_____

_____

_____

_____

_____

When I am fully ready to see what I see and know what I know

_____

_____

_____

_____

_____

_____

_____

_____

_____ 307

As I breathe deeply and feel my own power

_____

_____

_____

_____

_____

_____

_____

_____

When I look back at the distance I have traveled since beginning this book's sentence stems

_____

_____

_____

_____

_____

Right now it seems clear that

❧ Reflections ❧

_____

_____

_____

_____

_____

_____

_____

_____

_____

_____

_____

_____

_____

_____

_____

❧ *Reflections* ❧

Chapter 11

❧ ———————— ❧

Recommendations for Further Study

Although this is the most comprehensive set of sentence stems I have ever published, I am aware, as I draw to a conclusion, that I could easily have offered several hundred more. The possibilities are truly inexhaustible. On the other hand, the stems provided here are sufficient to keep a person working for quite a long time. If you do this book of stems again two months from now, many of your responses will be different. To repeat what I said near the beginning: Your sentence completions will usually be different if you repeat the same sentence stems at different times. The reason is that, in the course of doing this work, you have changed. You are now at another level of development.

If you repeated the entire procedure every two or three months for a year or two, you would keep on making new discoveries and encountering new surprises. I know—because I have done it and so have my therapy clients.

If you study the stems you will probably gather that a rather complex theory of psychology in general, and motivation in particular, is implicit in them. If you are interested in the wider picture, I refer you to books of mine already mentioned in the text: *Honoring the Self, The Psychology of Self-Esteem,* and *The Disowned Self.* For my views concerning love, sex, and man/woman relationships, I refer you to *The Psychology of Romantic Love* and *The Romantic Love Question & Answer Book* (written with E. Devers Branden). For the application of sentence completion to problems of communication in intimate relationships, read *"If You Could Hear What I Cannot Say."* If you resonate to the implicit philosophy of this book and wish to carry your self-work further, these books are the place to begin.

In addition, I have been developing a series of personal growth audiocassettes, aimed specifically at carrying forward in new ways the kind of learnings this workbook is designed to stimulate. You may obtain information about this program by writing to: The Biocentric Institute, P.O. Box 4009, Beverly Hills, California 90213.

I would be very happy to hear from you concerning your experiences with this workbook. Your feedback can help make the next one better.

If you were in my office and were working with sentence completion and hit a series of endings that agitated and confused you, I would say something like: "Breathe. Be a witness to your own feelings without being swallowed up by them. Allow the process to continue—and learn how much stronger you are than you think you are . . . how much more you know than you think you know . . . how much more you can do than you think you can do."

That is what I say to you now.

Appendix:

❧ ─────────── ❧

The Sentence Stems

Here is a list of the stems used in this book and the pages on which they appear.

ABOUT THE AUTHOR

Author of THE PSYCHOLOGY OF SELF-ESTEEM, BREAKING FREE, THE DISOWNED SELF, THE PSYCHOLOGY OF ROMANTIC LOVE, THE ROMANTIC LOVE QUESTION & ANSWER BOOK (with E. Devers Branden), "IF YOU COULD HEAR WHAT I CANNOT SAY," and HONORING THE SELF, NATHANIEL BRANDEN is a pioneer in his studies of self-esteem, personal transformation, and man/woman relationships. Dr. Branden is in private practice in Los Angeles and lives in Lake Arrowhead, California. Various books of his have been published in French, German, Portuguese, Dutch, Hebrew, Greek, Japanese, and Swedish.

As director of the Biocentric Institute in Los Angeles, he offers Intensive Workshops throughout the United States in self-esteem and man/woman relationships. He also conducts professional training workshops for mental health professionals in his approach to personal growth and development.

Communications to Dr. Branden or requests for information about his various lectures, seminars, and Intensive Workshops should be addressed to The Biocentric Institute, P.O. Box 4009, Beverly Hills, CA 90213.